My Story

Mission: To Proclaim Transformation and Truth

Published by: Transformed Publishing
Website: www.transformedpublishing.com
Email: transformedpublishing@gmail.com

Copyright © 2020 by Tawnya J. Jackson

All rights reserved solely by the author. No part of this book may be reproduced, stored in a retrieval system, or transmitted in any form or by any means without expressed written permission of the author.

Cover photography provided by MR-AH Photography.

Unless otherwise noted, scripture is taken from the King James Version. Public Domain.

As noted, scripture is taken from the New King James Version ®. Copyright © 1982 by Thomas Nelson. Used by permission. All rights reserved.

ISBN: 978-1-953241-02-3
Printed in the U.S.A.

My Story

How God Delivered, Healed, & Set Me Free

by Tawnya J. Jackson

Table of Contents

Foreword _____ vi

Dedication _____ viii

Introduction _____ 1

Chapter 1: Single Mother _____ 3

Chapter 2: Tired of Being Sick & Tired _____ 7

Chapter 3: Depressed _____ 9

Chapter 4: Pregnant _____ 11

Chapter 5: Choices _____ 13

Chapter 6: New Start _____ 17

Chapter 7: Bittersweet _____ 19

Chapter 8: Moving On _____ 23

Chapter 9: My God _____ 27

Chapter 10: Changes _____ 29

Chapter 11: Devastation _____ 33

Chapter 12: Death _____ 37

Chapter 13: Recovery _____ 41

Chapter 14: Smoke _____ 51

Chapter 15: Fire _____ 57

Chapter 16: Furnace _____ 63

Epilogue _____ 73

Fuel 10-Day Devotional _____ 77

Foreword

Written by Minister Rumika Knight

Prophetess, a title not loosely given, yet describing the very essence of Tawnya Jackson's life. When one truly walks in the prophetic office their lives become the object lesson to what God wants to reveal in the earth realm and teach to those who are humble enough to listen, receive, and learn.

A heart of gold she has, as she opens her arms to all those needing an embrace, a word of encouragement, or prayer. Tawnya places a high value on words, therefore she does not speak idly, hastily, or irresponsibly. A true friend indeed, always responding with the words, "Let me see what I can do," in translation, "Let me go consult the Lord for you!" Readily making herself available to carry the burdens of many, she spends hours in intercession throughout the week crying out to God for healing, covering, deliverance, and provision for all those placed upon her heart by the Holy Spirit.

Throughout the decades, Tawnya has learned how to truly live and has grown in her appreciation for life. Her many experiences have afforded her the right to sympathetically dish out wisdom whenever deemed necessary. One would benefit greatly to listen and obey.

Her motherlike nature has nurtured many to spiritual, mental, and emotional health. There is a Grace that exists which is connected to the tangibility of the reality of who the God of Jesus the Christ is. Tawnya possesses that Grace. There is only one God.

Ever so meek, Tawnya is anointed to make known the mystery of the living God. Her life answers the questions of God's purposeful involvement in the lives of those who seek Him. Her triumphant victories tell the story of God's continuous love for mankind. Her faith, as she ever so prophetically declares over her life and the lives of others, is a constant reminder of God's willingness to not only carry our burdens, but that we may know He always has our backs, and He is always there for us!

> ["]Be strong and of good courage, do not fear nor be afraid of them; for the LORD your God, He *is* the One who goes with you. He will not leave you nor forsake you."
>
> Deuteronomy 31:6

Dedication

I dedicate this book to my sister Kimberly LaShawn Rogers Glenn, who passed away in 2008. She was my mentor, my inspiration, and my confidant.

Kim continuously encouraged me by saying, "Tawnya, write the book!" My sister taught me so much! I never got the chance to tell her how much she made a difference in my life and how she was a great example of how to be a profound big sister in her younger sister's life. She prayed for me when I was in *the world* doing everything *I was big and bad enough to do*. She never judged me.

**Kimberly LaShawn Rogers Glenn
9/25/1964 – 11/23/2008**

I will always love you Kim with all my heart. I pray I have made you proud. Here is my first book, which I dedicate to you!

Sisters Forever!

I also dedicate this book to my four daughters Sha'Therian, Sha'Tawnya, ShaTalya, and Donajia. I want you all to know that I love you with all of my heart and soul!

I wish being a parent would have come with a handbook. I realize now that there were so many mistakes I made, and I wish I would've done many things differently. I pray you all can find it in your hearts, if you haven't already, to forgive me. I am so sorry for any pain I may have caused.

I want you all to know, God could not have given me greater children than each of you! Thank you for being the greatest daughters a mother could ever ask for. The four of you are so brilliant, beautiful, strong, and special in so many ways.

Mommy will always love you!

Introduction

What a beautiful Saturday morning God has blessed me to see! I am laying across my bed thinking about how grateful I am to the Lord. He has brought me a long way over the years.

Let's drift down memory lane together back to the 1990's. At that time, I was the mother of three daughters, divorced, living the single life, and had done everything *I was big and bad enough to do*. Yes, that included drugs, alcohol, dating a married man, partying all night, not working, and living off of government assistance and child support.

Eventually, I came to a point in my life where *I was tired of being sick and tired.* I wanted change. I had my entire life ahead of me. I had ambitions and desires. Unfortunately, I did not know how to bring them to pass, so I continued to live two lives. I was miserable and unhappy but continued to do whatever it took to get from one day to the next.

1
Single Mother

Year: 1993

Sha'Therian (Tori) and Sha'Tawnya (Tia) are my oldest two daughters. At this time, ShaTalya was the youngest. She was spoiled and always whining. Being the oldest, Tori was so humble and cared for her younger sisters and even me sometimes when I was tired from getting high or depressed. All the drama I went through with Donald, my boyfriend at the time who I started dating when ShaTalya was eight months old, took a toll on me.

Donald was a married man when I started to date him. He was also a longtime family friend, who I never thought I would have an interest in. When I said *yes* to this relationship, all hell broke out. I learned how to accept the good with the bad when it came to Donald. We broke up many times over the years just to make up. It was foolishness. His wife finally divorced him. The divorce was not directly because of me, but I am sure myself and the other women he fooled around with played a great part in it.

Life went on. I have the best supportive family in the world. My mom has always been a great mother. She took care of her three children. She raised us up right and took, or sent us, to church on Sundays. Even when she did not go, she still sent us. She made sure we were dressed in the best. Her children have always been her everything and she loves us very much.

My daddy was *The Man*. True to the saying, *Papa was a rolling stone, wherever he laid his hat was his home.* He has about twenty children that I know of, but rumors say there are even more. I loved my father with all my heart and soul. He was a great man. He always provided for his family and made sure there was a roof over our heads and meals on the table each day. We never went without lights and water. I thank God for my parents.

My sister Kim, who is the oldest, and I were always so different and distant. She was slow when it came to the streets; she did not know anything about the fast life. I always said she was a *holy roller.* Honey, she was so geeky. I always loved her so much and admired how intelligent and independent she was. *Organized* was really her first name.

Oh Lord, then there is my brother Byron who I love so very much but could not stand some of his ways. Byron and I are ten months apart in age. I am older, even though he always thought he was Kim and I's daddy; especially mine. *Tell the truth and shame the devil,* Byron would steal the sweetness out of your sugar and then lie about it to the end. In spite of that, I love my brother. He is such a big teddy bear.

Those are my family members. Yes, my wonderful family whom I love! We have had a lot of drama over the years, but we always *nip it in the butt* and get things back on track.

My family never knew about the drugs I did. They knew I drank sociably and smoked a little weed. My reasoning was, *I'm grown.* They did not know about my cocaine snorting habit, which I called *my social entertainment.* My motto was, *I do the dope; it doesn't do me.* Yeah right.

2
Tired of Being Sick & Tired

Year: 1994

At this point, I was just *tired of being sick and tired* of not fulfilling my dreams. I felt like I was not being the best mom I could be to my daughters, even though they have always been my number one priority. I love them so much! They are wonderful girls and have never given me any problems. I wouldn't allow it. No matter what I did, I made sure my girls were well taken care of. I would send them to church even if I did not go. *See the pattern?* I got that from my mommy. They were honor roll students, well-behaved, and dressed in the best. I really love my children with all my heart, and I showed them the best I knew how. *Was it good enough?* I don't know.

I kept a lot of my mess out in the streets where it belonged. I did not bring it home to my kids. I always prayed and told God, *if my drug and alcohol use ever come to the point where it's going to affect my children in any way, take it away Lord.*

I continued to be a mom and date Donald. I continued using drugs and alcohol. I was not happy. There was a void in my life.

Every time I thought *maybe this, maybe that,* or *maybe him* will eventually fill the never-ending void I carried, I was again disappointed. It came to the point where partying was no longer exciting, and my friends were no more fun. Donald was cheating more than ever, or should I say, I started finding out more about Donald's cheating. My girls started looking at me like they knew all about my mess and hang-ups. I felt like I was not good enough for anyone; not even myself. The weight of depression overtook me like an avalanche.

3
Depressed

Year: 1999-2000

Consumed by the stronghold of depression, I sat in a dark house all day and night. I was not getting dressed or fixing my hair. I now call it foolishness, but at that time in my life, it was my reality. Tori was about fourteen years old. She kept the house clean, cooked, and took care of her two sisters. She was being the mom.

Not many people knew about the double life I was living for fifteen years, not even my ex-husband. Yes, the man I was married to knew nothing about my cocaine snorting habit, or as I reasoned it, *my social entertainment*.

My sister Kim had moved away to Palm Bay, FL, located about two hours north of where I was living. I was happy that I could get away with my girls, so we visited her regularly. Whenever I was there, I could think clearly. It was an opportunity to visualize and dream again while away from all the drama. I did not even want to get high or drink. It was so peaceful. I enjoyed going to church, family get-togethers, and hearing my daughters laugh while we were there. Seeing the fun they had, really brought joy to my heart. As soon as I returned home though, it was back to the drawing board.

4
Pregnant

June 2001

I found out I was pregnant by Donald. At first, I thought I was experiencing menopause because a baby was the last thing on my mind. Nevertheless, I took a pregnancy test, and it was confirmed - *I was definitely pregnant!*

In the beginning, I was in shock. Then, after a few days, I was okay. The time had come to face reality. I told Donald. His immediate response was, "Stop playing Tawnya!" After he saw I was serious, he stepped right up, "Everything is going to be okay. It is alright. We got to do what we got to do."

Hope arose. *Maybe he will get it right. Maybe he will stop messing around with other women.* One thing I knew with surety was that Donald loved my daughters and I very much. He never treated them like they were not his natural daughters. That is one reason I loved him so much.

We never lived together. I made a commitment after my divorce that no man would lay up in my house with my daughters and I unless we were married. However, I did make an exception for Donald and let him stay the night on occasion. I thought maybe the baby would change both of our lives. Maybe we would even get married. None of these things happened right away.

5
Choices

Depressed. Crying. Yelling. Cursing. I hated Donald. I always ran him off. Even if he stopped cheating, I just assumed he started back. I accused him of cheating with every woman who looked in his direction.

All that was just a bunch of drama. I did not want to be pregnant at this time in my life, so I would get mad and go to Palm Bay to visit my sister. Whenever I was there, my attitude and everything else changed. I rested in peace without all the madness going on.

During one particular visit, I started seeking an apartment. At this time, I was about six months pregnant. No one back home, not even Donald, knew what I was doing. I was looking out for what was best for me and my children.

Contrary to my actions when away from home, as soon as I got back in town to Donald, I no longer wanted to move. It ended up being his *week* to love on me. He took me shopping; both for myself and the baby. He bought a car seat, a walker, a stroller, and a highchair. In fact, whatever my hand touched, he bought. This is something he always did. He had me *acting like somebody!*

December 2001

I received a phone call notifying me that I had been approved for the apartment in Palm Bay. I started saying little things to Donald about how I would like to move. Donald was not hearing any of that. He said he was not moving anywhere, and neither was I. He wasn't leaving the Fort Lauderdale and Pompano Beach area because he had to work, and nor was I with his baby. His exact words were, "Tawnya, you have really gone crazy. I told you woman, CRAZY!"

We were together so much; he was *tripping over me.* I was thinking, *he really loves me. Child, please.* Just one week later, I saw that joker with my own eyes talking to another woman. They were too close for comfort.

My mind was racing. *Oh, that was it! This negro had tried me for the last time!* To keep myself from going to jail, I went home and called my parents. They moved to Palm Bay two months prior to this incident. I told them to come get me and my three now because I am leaving Donald and all his mess right here. My mom and dad loved the ground Donald walked on. They did not know the half about him. Honey, I was ready to sound the alarm and tell everything from the beginning to the end about that joker.

I did not tell Donald about what I saw or what I was doing. I stopped accepting his phone calls and would not answer the door. I packed up everything I owned into a moving truck. I did like The Beverly Hillbillies and *I got out of Dodge.*

February 2002

On February 14, 2002, I came back to Ft. Lauderdale to turn in my keys to the landlord. I told Donald I would be in town that day at 10 a.m. He met me there. I was with my parents. He came to the van with the biggest Valentine's gift basket I had ever seen. He had someone make it especially for me. He kissed me on the cheek and said he will always love me. Then he walked away. That was one of the saddest days of my life. My heart felt like it was broken in half, but I believed that if he loved me, he would get it together and pursue me.

6
New Start

I went to Palm Bay and started my life all over again. I attended church. I enrolled my daughters in their new schools. I continually prayed for God to disconnect me from my past experiences.

March 2002

March 17, 2002, I had my beautiful baby Donajia. She looked just like her daddy. Donald was there in the delivery room. My sister had called to tell him my water broke and in the next hour and forty-five minutes he was there.

Donald loved Donajia so much. He would come to Palm Bay about four days out of the week and drive back the same night. I was serious that either he was going to do things the right way or not at all.

Donald claimed he had changed, but deep in my heart I knew better. I was trying to focus on myself. I had given my life to Christ again. My daughters were praise dancing in church and all over the community. God was really blessing me in so many areas of my life. I made new friends at church. The things I used to do; I wasn't doing anymore. I faithfully read my bible daily, prayed, went to church, and was not sexing Donald.

Suddenly, out of the blue, I wanted a twenty-cent piece of powder just to chill out. *You know the Word of God says He is a forgiving God.* That is what the enemy was telling me. *Just confess your sins. It's alright.*

After I finished doing it, I felt so ashamed. *How did I get here?* One thing I knew was I did not want to go back to where I came from. I got on my knees. I cried and prayed; however, this would not be my last time succumbing to temptation.

7
Bittersweet

Year: 2003

A full year passed. Donald visited on the weekends and we all went to church together. On Sunday nights, he traveled back to Pompano Beach for work. Honey, I'm not crazy, but I was sure he was doing more than working. Some nights I called his cell phone and he wouldn't answer. I knew he was up to no good. Nonetheless, I had to stay focused on what God was doing in my life. Paying too much attention to his nonsense would have caused me to lose focus.

God blessed me to move into my first house. Yes, Donald still supported us. That is one of the things he did well. That is why I put up with his foolishness. Momma has said: *A piece of a man is better than no man; especially if he is giving you money and paying your bills.* The devil is a liar. Many days I wished I would have paid my own bills and dumped Donald, but I loved that man, I am not going to lie!

By this time, Tori and Tia were in high school and growing up to be such beautiful young ladies. They still never gave me much trouble at all. I knew that neither one of them was crazy, in fact, both are very intelligent.

As they watched and listened to everything, they wanted to know *why* I put up with Donald. Some woman had called the house for him and they did not tell me. They gave him the phone to speak with her. Supposedly, it was his cousin. After the fact, I found out about this.

My girls, Tori and Tia, started to spend a lot of time in their bedroom when Donald would come into town. They made themselves scarce. I noticed the difference but reasoned to myself, *this is my life and it isn't bad at all. It could be a lot worse.* When I would cook dinner, they would not come out to the table to eat as a family. I assumed they did not want to be a part of this *fairy tale family*. Donald went out of his way to buy and do things for them to make them happy, but they weren't four and six years old anymore. They knew their mother deserved better than this.

One particular weekend, they ticked me off with the way they treated Donald. When he left to go back to Pompano Beach, I wanted everyone center floor in the living room.

"Tori and Tia, come here now!" I yelled. "What is going on?"

Their response was, "Nothing."

"Oh yeah, something is going on. Why are you two acting like that with Donald? When he speaks, you all act like you can barely move your mouths. He is trying to hold a conversation, but you all have nothing to say." The more questions I asked, the less chance I gave them to respond.

I slowed down and changed my line of questioning to make sure they were not in danger. "Has he touched you all the wrong way?"

They replied, "No."

"Has he mistreated you all or said something he shouldn't have?"

They again replied, "No."

"Okay, listen to me. Donald is my boyfriend. He takes care of this household. He does just as much as your daddy does for the both of you. Stop tripping because he is not going anywhere! As long as he doesn't touch you inappropriately, mistreat you all, or verbally abuse you; when he talks to you, you better open your mouths. That is respect. You will respect him in this house. If you don't like it or you feel I am wrong, then go to your daddy."

"That's not fair!" Tori protested.

"I tell you what, I will not be repeating myself." That was the end of that episode.

8
Moving On

Year: 2004

My daughter ShaTalya was spoiled. Give her a TV, a PlayStation game, and something from McDonald's; and she was fine. Her and Donald were *two peas in a pot.* He raised her and provided for her since she was eight months old. He was the father figure in her life.

One of the happiest days of my life was in May 2004. My first-born daughter Tori graduated from high school with her Associates of Art Degree. I definitely was and continue to be a proud mother! Both her father and Donald came into town for the celebration.

My ex-husband, Theron, is a great dad. He has always been the provider and supporter of my oldest two daughters, Tori and Tia. He went over and beyond just paying child support all the time. Donald and Theron got along good for the children's sake, yet I knew they really did not like each other. We always did things as a family when it involved the girls.

I still went to church faithfully. Truthfully, I was *playing church.* As soon as I got home on Sundays, I went to the bathroom to smoke a cigarette. Yes, I hid from my girls – *like cigarette smoke doesn't smell.*

My friend from back home in Ft. Lauderdale, would call me to tell me about parties she was having and talk all about everything I had stopped doing. Sure enough, I started going back and forth to Ft. Lauderdale. As soon as I was done, I came back to Palm Bay crying and repenting. I learned that I was not strong enough to go back into those territories.

I had to make a quality decision to stop going to visit my old friends. To live a changed life, I had to let old things pass away. So, when my friend would call, I started to say *no*. I did not want to tell her the real reason, so I would say that I had to go to church or something.

In actuality, I was tired of playing with God. He had been so good to me and my family. I was seriously ready to get to know who He is. I spent most of my life in church and still did not really know God. I wanted a genuine relationship with Him. I was tired of seeing myself before the Lord apologizing for the same sins over and over. I presented the same repetitive list: sex outside of marriage, drinking, and getting high.

I started to build a relationship with the Lord. This was something I never had before. I started to fall in love with Jesus.

The Lord truly became my Father and my Friend. He protected me and provided for me.

At this point in my life, I had kicked Donald to the curb. He wanted to get married, but it was not the right time for me.

9
My God

I could tell the Lord anything and He would listen. I started to spend time with the Lord in the midnight hours: praising Him, worshipping Him, and reading His Word. A lot of things I read did not make sense. I prayed and asked for understanding, wisdom, and knowledge of the Word. God started to give me what I had been praying for. My time with the Lord became more exciting and fun. It was not as hard as I thought it would be.

I began to hear from God. I received instructions that had to do with specific people and what to do about certain situations. This really became serious. I loved it because all the negative things started to move out of my life. I became a positive person with a new mindset.

I knew the church I was currently a part of could not take me where I was going. I outgrew it there. I stopped going to church for a couple of months. There was a church in my heart I wanted to attend. The enemy taunted me by saying *they are going to say you left that church to go to that other church.* I knew that the pastors knew each other, so that reinforced the negative thought.

I found a new friend and His name is Jesus. Sometimes I stayed up all night to watch the gospel channel. I listened to the men and women of God teach and preach the Word. My hunger and thirst for the Lord led me to pray and praise all night long. I wanted to know everything about Him. Once I got the girls ready for school and out the door in the morning, I went to bed and slept for a couple of hours. When I woke up, I continued to praise the Lord. I became a true worshiper. I loved Jesus!

Life became so wonderful for me. We would get the whole family together, along with my mom, dad, Kim, and her children. We packed lunch and went fishing all day until late at night when the mosquitoes started biting. We did not care because we were having so much fun. There was a lot to do in the community: The Strawberry Festival, Art Festival, Seafood Festival, Gospel Explosion, Black Historical Marches, and more. We loved exploring the area. There was always something to do that was either cheap or free. *Yes, God is good all the time.*

10
Changes

Finally, the chance came for me to visit the church my heart desired. My life was going great. I joined a new ministry. My children were doing well.

Because of the teaching I now received and the relationship I developed with God, I started to feel more convicted of sin. It was no longer so easy, or should I say *comfortable,* to sin. Donald and I were still together but I did not play about all that sexing and shacking. It seemed like every Sunday, Apostle said something about shacking or having sex outside of marriage. I thought God showed him my life and if I did anything, he was able to see it. I told Donald, "I'm not playing with God. If you stay the weekend, you can't touch me because I'm saved *for real."*

His response was, "Keep listening to the damn preacher around that corner and you're going to be by yourself!"

I prayed and asked God to change Donald. I needed clarity and action. *If Donald was going to marry me, then let him marry me; but if not, then please move him completely out of my life.*

My father was eighty-six years old and in good health. He never complained about anything other than arthritis pain in his hands and knees. Out of the blue, my father had a stroke. I prayed and asked God to save my family. The Lord told me He was going to save my father and my brother.

The hospital called and told me, after I visited my father that same day, there had been a code blue. I stood in my kitchen crying out to the Lord saying, "God, You promised me You were going to save my daddy! Now, I believe Your Word and it can't return unto You void."

The hospital called me back to let me know that my father had been revived and was stable. I will never forget when my family and I got to the hospital to see my father. He was just glowing and smiling. He was overjoyed to tell us about the near-death experience he had with the Lord. He wanted to tell everyone he came in contact with *to get their lives right with the Lord.*

This is my father's story:

He was asleep in some type of white chariot. He woke up when the chariot stopped. He arose to such beautiful singing; it was the angels. *Everything* was more beautiful than *anything* his eyes had ever seen! There were even mansions. When he went to step out of the chariot, three men in white robes stood before him and said, "No, you can't come now. You must go back and tell your family to get their lives together."

My daddy set up meetings with all of us. He talked to us individually and told us what the Lord had said. Family and friends traveled for miles to hear my father's testimony. Every time he told the story tears fell down his face. Never before, did I see my daddy cry like this. It really touched his heart, and I knew he was changed by this experience. God had done just what He promised. He saved my daddy!

Over the next week, as people came and went, they asked my daddy if he wanted prayer. Daddy said firmly, "No, I don't want to stay here. I want to go back to where I was. I just came to tell my family and everyone else, to get their lives right with the Lord. I'm ready to go back."

After we brought him home to my sister's house for about two to three days, my father had a massive stroke and was put on life support. We knew, deep down inside, after this he was not coming back. We laid my daddy to rest. This was one of the hardest things I ever had to do in my life. I was definitely a daddy's girl; a piece of my heart was gone.

February 2007

Finally, the time had come! Donald asked me to marry him. He had said *it* so many times that I didn't even take him seriously. I said, "Okay, let me know when you're ready."

"I'm ready now," he said.

Each day Donald reminded me, "Tawnya, I'm serious."

My response was, "Okay."

While I was at work one day, Donald called me to say he was picking me up during my lunch break. He did. He said again, "Tawnya, I want you to be my wife."

"Okay Donald. You have to put action behind your words."

"Okay Tawnya. Today after work we are going to the courthouse."

I returned to work and told my two friends what Donald said. They were screaming and jumping with excitement, but I told them, "I will believe it when I see it."

I received a call before I clocked out of work from Donald. He said he was going to pick up Donajia from school and he wanted me to pick up ShaTalya, then meet him at the courthouse. That day, I became Mrs. Jackson.

Our family, church family, and friends, were so happy for us but they were mad because no one had been invited to the wedding. I told them it happened so quick; I did not have a chance to call anyone.

11
Devastation

Year: 2008

My sister Kim taught Bible Study to the Youth Department. One night she was wrapped up in a blanket in her classroom. I asked her, "What is the matter?"

She responded, "I'm cold and have chills."

The elders of the church prayed for her. The next day she was hospitalized. The doctors could not find out what was wrong with her. Eventually, she was diagnosed with leukemia and needed a bone marrow transplant. They discussed transferring her to another hospital in Tampa, FL for surgery. Nevertheless, before a plan was finalized, they concluded it would be impossible to do the surgery.

For months, my sister was hospitalized. I ran back and forth every day to make sure she was taken care of properly. Little by little, we noticed that some things were not getting done if we were not there. I spoke with my husband to see if it was okay with him for me to stop working. For my sister to receive the proper care she needed, I realized I had to be there. I already knew what Donald's answer would be. Out of respect, I asked anyway and just as I thought, he said, "Of course, go ahead and do what you have to do."

I prayed and believed God for total healing for my sister. I stood on the Word of God and I was full of faith. I would not let any negativity around her in the hospital. I believed God for a miracle.

I cared for my family at home and my sister in the hospital. I also checked on my sister's children and my mom. I continued to go to every church service.

During all this, my husband had complained several times about a small knot in his stomach. One day he took my hand and put it on his stomach. I felt a little hard lump. I snatched my hand away and exclaimed, "What is that? You need to go to the doctor and see about this!"

He responded, "I have to work. I don't want to run up no hospital bills."

"I don't care nothing about no hospital bills! I care about you, my husband, and that's all!"

Every time I would bring it up, he would argue, "I don't have time to lay up in no hospital. I have to take care of my family. Who is going to pay these bills, Tawnya?"

That is when the Holy Spirit told me, "Be quiet and don't mention it anymore. Just pray." That is what I did.

One night I was praying in the family room and I fell asleep. I knew Donald had to get up early for work, so I did not want to disturb him. Around midnight my daughter ShaTalya woke me up and said, "Mommy, Donald said come here. He is not feeling well."

I jumped up and ran into the room. Donald was bent over holding his stomach in pain. I directed him to get dressed in order to go to the hospital. He started to get dressed and I thought, *Thank You Jesus!*

We sat in the emergency room from 1 a.m. to 7 a.m. laughing and talking about everything. Then without warning, in an instant, everything changed. A team of doctors walked in the room and told us my husband had stage four bladder cancer.

I looked in his eyes and saw the tears he was trying to hold back. With all sincerity, I looked at him and said, "We got this!"

I told Donald I had to step outside of the room to make a phone call because the reception in the hospital was bad. As I walked down the hallways, they seemed so long, like they would never end. I finally made it outside and exploded. I screamed at the top of my lungs, "No God! Why?"

People walked by and looked at me like I was crazy. I dropped to the curbside and cried. I sat there until I was able to stand up and walk back to the room where my husband was.

Donald's only concern was *if I was alright.*

I assured him, "I'm good. How are you?"

Words of strength and hope arose from my husband, "I'm okay. It is not over!"

I continued to take care of everybody else and neglected myself. My sister and my husband were on the same floor of the hospital for weeks.

12
Death

Year: 2008 - 2009

After months of receiving chemotherapy, my sister Kim passed away in November 2008. My husband Donald passed away in June 2009.

The hospital called me one morning and said, "Mrs. Jackson, if you don't come now, you..."

Before the sentence was finished, I just said, "Okay." I hung up the phone. All night I had prayed. I prayed for a miracle but did not receive peace. I knew what that meant.

I dropped my two youngest daughters off at my mom's house. My mother wanted to come with me to see Donald, but I did not want her to know what was going on at this time because she had her own health issues.

I arrived at the hospital, entered Donald's room, and stood at the side of his bed. I told him how much I loved and appreciated him for everything. I let him know it was okay for him to go to take his rest and to tell my dad, my sister, his mother, and his stepfather *hello* for me. I assured him not to worry about me and his family.

We would be alright. I mentioned this because Donald and some of his family members had been going back and forth over some issues concerning me. People will dislike you without knowing what is going on. Donald was tired of the bickering and all the foolishness.

I continued to let him know how much I loved him. I kissed my husband and sat down in the chair. I did not want to *fall out.* I wanted to be strong until the end for him. I sat there for about fifteen minutes. Then I heard the heart monitor blare out a loud still noise.

The nurse ran into the room. As soon as she said my name, "Mrs. Jackson," I replied, "I know" and waved my hand to motion for her to leave. I just cried and cried. I was so hurt. My heart felt like it had broken into pieces. I sat there until I felt I had enough strength to walk and drive. I wanted to hold my babies in my arms.

The nurse asked me if I needed her to call someone for me. I did not feel like talking and having to answer questions, so I told her, "No thank you."

I was distraught as I pulled back the curtain to walk out of my husband's ICU room. I looked directly into my mother's face. "What are you doing here?"

"I wanted to see Donald. Where is he?"

"Momma, Donald just died."

My mother let out a piercing scream.

I tried to comfort her, "Momma!"

She continued to scream, "Tawnya! It hurts so bad. There is a pain in my head."

The nurses ran over and asked, "What is going on?"

I was numb. *My momma. Not now. I can't handle anymore.*

They immediately rushed my mother to the emergency room downstairs. She was given a diagnosis - a brain aneurysm.

13

Recovery

My children have continued to excel and make me a proud parent. Tia graduated high school in 2006 and had to make a choice between going to the Air Force or Job Corps. In 2007, she eventually decided to go to Job Corps because she really did not want to go to college. I wanted her to go to the Air Force like her dad did. I really believed that was what she wanted too, but at that time, someone else had a greater influence on her than her parents. Tia was in Job Corps when both Kim and Donald died. She flew home both times to attend their funerals.

I thank God for the experiences she had at Job Corps. She earned a promotion to dorm room monitor and instead of sharing a room with four to six other young ladies, she only had one roommate. Tia graduated with her Pharmacy Technician Certification.

Things started to come together in my life once again. I wanted something for me, so I started to volunteer my time cleaning the church. I really enjoyed it. I went a few days out of the week and prayed and praised while I cleaned.

Normally I was alone in the sanctuary because the daycare was on the other side of the church. I was not trying to go over there because I felt I had volunteered enough time with those little soldiers. I loved when I was in the sanctuary. I kneeled at the altar or laid and casted all of my cares upon God. I needed Him. This time in my life was not easy for me. I was still in the beginning stages of trying to get myself *back into the swing of things*. I cried out to the Lord to ask for help with *all* my situations. I prayed for my leaders, my church family, and everyone else God laid on my heart. When I finished praying, I always felt so much better. I praised Him as I vacuumed and dusted to welcome the Presence of God into the place. I did this for several weeks. During that time, I received money, checks, and other blessings coming from everywhere. I did not have a job. As I volunteered in God's house, He caused men to pour unto me.

The days I volunteered at the church, I always had to leave before 2:00 p.m. to pick up my youngest daughter from the bus stop after school. My usual routine was to leave the church at 1:55 p.m., go pick up Donajia from her bus stop, and then go home. Our house was just a few houses down from her bus stop.

One day, as Donajia and I drove up to the house, I was talking on the phone to my dear sister Kia from church. Like we always did, we talked about the goodness of the Lord. I unlocked the front door of my house. My mouth dropped. My house was definitely not how I left it. Everything was thrown everywhere. I told sister Kia I had to call her back because my house had been broken into. I hung up and told my daughter to stay outside by the front door.

I walked down the hallway slowly so I could see more of the house. When I approached the family room, I glanced over towards the two bedrooms. Immediately I became afraid. *Is someone still inside?* I ran outside to the middle of the street and called 911. I told the dispatcher what happened. The dispatcher advised me that an officer was on the way and to please not go back inside because someone might still be in there. I said to myself, *you don't have to tell me twice.*

As I waited for the officer, it seemed like a lifetime passed. I knocked on a couple of my neighbors' doors and asked them if they had seen anything. They could not believe what I was saying because our neighborhood was quiet and nice. No one had seen or heard anything.

Finally, the police arrived. I approached the officer and explained to him what I came home to. He told me to stay outside because it was possible, I came home before they could get out. He drew his weapon to go inside.

"Don't worry about me. You go ahead. I will be here when you get back."

The officer returned and said, "It is clear, but you have a mess inside."

The officer and I walked back into the house. I was so angry and afraid at the same time. I never imagined in the forty something years of my life that I would be a victim of crime; especially not my house being broken into.

Once again, I was numb. I could not believe what I saw. I was speechless. My house was so organized when I left home that morning and it now looked like an illustration for the expression, *trying to find a needle in a haystack.*

Oh my God, what was I going to do? I wanted to walk out and never look back at this mess. The officer had called my name about four times. Suddenly his voice penetrated my racing thoughts.

"Mrs. Jackson. Mrs. Jackson. Will you please try to look around and see what is missing? I know you are going to need a couple of days before you can really determine everything that is missing, but we need to start the report."

Where should I even begin? I began to walk through the house. I stepped over the dresser drawers which had been dumped out and the mattress that was pulled to the floor. My clothes, that I always took the time to sort and arrange neatly in my walk-in closet, were now thrown everywhere. My shoes were even in my bathroom toilet and bathtub! They must have gotten in by breaking through the master bedroom bathroom window.

It seemed as if someone had thrown my house up in the air and wherever the stuff landed, that is where it now was. I really thought it was *impossible* to clean up. I was so mad! *I always worked so hard to keep my house clean and organized just for someone to come in and vandalize it.*

My neighbors came to see what happened. They were amazed at what they saw because we thought our neighborhood was safe, but we all got a rude awakening. Shockingly, such a horrendous act took place right outside of their front doors.

My anger launched my thoughts in *crazy* directions. *How is it that no one saw anything in the broad daylight? Are they trying to run me out of the neighborhood because I am black? Out of all the houses in this neighborhood, why was my house chosen when there are so many others to choose from?*

Right away, I noticed that the cases from our electronic devices were thrown everywhere. They had taken our digital camera, portable DVD player, PlayStation with the games, an iPod, and my husband's watches and cufflinks that I had kept for keepsakes. The police officer made a report and dusted for fingerprints. As we talked, he informed me, over the last several weeks numerous break-ins involving teenagers were reported in the area. The teenagers randomly approached houses and knocked or rang the doorbell. If no one answered, they went to the back of the house to break in.

I prayed and told the Lord to catch every last one of them. They needed to be punished, counseled, and taught to do better before they go into the wrong house where someone is inside waiting with a gun and a life is taken.

I was really afraid to stay home that night. My mom and I boarded up the broken window. The window company was not able to replace the window until the next day. I knew if I did not face my fears that first night, I would not be able to return there and live peacefully. My daughters were afraid for months, but I thank God things got better as time passed.

One of my neighbors, who I had not spoken to yet about the break-in, came by a couple of days later. She gave me some important information. Around 1:00 p.m. that day, she saw four black boys on bikes come from the back of my house with big backpacks. She was suspicious because at that time of day, kids were still supposed to be at school. However, she minimized the thought, since she always saw children visiting my home; she reasoned they belonged there.

I provided the officer investigating my case with this information. Three weeks later the detective called. They confiscated some of my belongings and arrested all the suspects that were involved. I got back what was important to me; specifically, some of things that belonged to my husband. Everything else was replaceable. I was grateful. God did what I asked. Each one of the young men was incarcerated for over a year. I prayed their lives would change.

God continued to prove Himself amazing. Just one month after the break-in, my home did not look like what had taken place there. It almost seemed like it never happened. Everything was back into place and organized like it was before. *What an awesome God we serve! He makes all things new.*

My family members continued to move forward in a positive direction. My mom was doing much better. She loves the outdoors and was again able to take care of the flowers in her yard. She even planted a garden. It was so good to see her return to doing the things she enjoys. More so, being able to do what she wants when she wants to. My mom has always been a very independent woman.

I began to notice that it was getting difficult for her to remember some things. When we talked about certain places, she acted clueless, like she never had been there before. She would say, "Where was I when that happened?" It really frustrated her. Most of all, I think she was scared because parts of her life were fading away from her memory.

Overall, God had performed yet another miracle in my mother's life. Before the brain aneurism, she had a liver condition. At that time, doctors had also given up hope. Their verdict was that she would have to receive blood transfusions for the rest of her life and we should *just take her home*. Not so. God healed her body! She never had another blood transfusion, and the condition was gone.

I also have a distinct memory from my early teenage years, as I stood facing an operating room door, I looked on as doctors and nurses ran around during a code blue. They were losing my mother on the operating table during an emergency gallbladder surgery.

The same God who saved her life then and totally healed her body, was at work again! Not once, not twice, but three times! After the brain aneurism, my mother was back to cooking and cleaning. The doctor even said she would eventually be able to drive again.

God has repeatedly done what no man was able to do. When the doctors said *no,* God said *yes*! *Hallelujah!* I give God all the glory.

Excitement continued to build. I looked forward to what God had for me *now.* I accepted that I had to let go of my will in exchange for His will. Of course, I did not understand it all and why I went through everything I went through, but I made a quality decision to trust in the Lord. There was no way He brought me this far to leave me.

My sister Kim's children's names are Ebony, Brandis, and Elisha. She also has a granddaughter named Jordyn. All the children continued to excel: Tori, Tia, and Ebony were working. Brandis was still in college at FAMU. Elisha and ShaTalya both played basketball and they were great at it - very cocky though. They did not think the game could start until their feet hit the court. Jordyn and Donajia, *Lawd have mercy on them.* Jordyn loved Donajia when she didn't mind being bothered, but when Donajia got on her nerves, she was so mean to my baby and treated her like a stepchild. Donajia looked up to Jordyn so much, she would do anything Jordyn told her, *poor child.*

My brother Byron was also doing okay. I know he missed Daddy and Kim a lot, even though he tried to act tough. He tried to keep it all together, but deep down inside, I knew he was hurting. I diligently prayed that Byron would give his life to God. No one can fix *it* like Him. If I did not have the Lord on my side, honey, I have no idea and don't even want to think about where I would be. My nephew, Byron Jr. was doing well. Handsome just like his daddy and still living in Pompano Beach.

14
Smoke

Year: 2010

Tia walked into my bedroom and asked if she could use my car to go to the beauty supply store. She was getting her hair braided and they ran out of hair. I told her, "I don't care as long as you put gas in my car and be back before I have to leave to go to seven o'clock bible study."

"Okay Mom, I'll be back."

"I'm not playing. I don't want to be late for church."

She left. As I got ready for church, I praised the Lord. My girlfriend Annette called. We had a good time as we talked on the phone celebrating the goodness of the Lord. Some people refer to the telephone as the *hell-a-phone,* but I disagree. It depends on who you are talking to and what you are talking about. My best friend and I can talk for hours about the goodness of the Lord. No gossiping, no foolishness. Honey, God has been too good to the both of us.

It was about 6:15 p.m. and I told Annette, "Child, let me get off this phone and finish getting ready for church. I'll talk to you later when I get back home."

"Okay my friend." she replied, and we hung up.

Not even a minute later, the phone rang. It was Tia. "Girl, bring me my car." She knows I don't play with my car or about getting to church on time.

"Mommy, the police just stopped me."

"What happened?" I was shocked because Tia is a very responsible safe driver.

"Mommy, she said she wants Tawnya Jackson. She asked me, 'Who is she?'. I told her you are my mom. Then she asked where you were. I told her you were at home."

"Tia, what is she asking about me for? Don't tell that woman nothing else about me and bring my car home!" I hung up my phone. Honey, let me tell you, I am scared of trouble.

Immediately after I hung up, the phone rang again. My daughter said, "Mommy, she wants to talk to you."

"For what?"

The next thing I heard was the police officer's voice. "Mrs. Jackson?"

"Yes," I hesitantly replied.

The officer introduced herself.

"What do you want with me, officer?"

"There is a warrant for your arrest ma'am," the officer informed me.

"No dear. You have the wrong person."

She asked me to confirm my birthdate and address. "Yes, ma'am it is."

"Okay, well I do have the right person."

I began to plead my case. My voice trembled, "A warrant? For what? Listen officer, I am a Christian. I do not get into no trouble. I don't mess with you'll and definitely don't want you'll coalescing with me."

"Mrs. Jackson, that is what the computer is giving me."

"How did you find this information?"

The officer explained, "I am assigned to an undercover task force. I run license plates in search of people with outstanding warrants. Mrs. Jackson, are you home now?"

"Yes."

"Well, I'll just come over now and take you in so we can get all this straightened out."

This cannot be happening. I earnestly needed the truth to arise in this situation. "The devil is a liar. You are not coming to where I live. I have neighbors. I am a woman of integrity. You have made a mistake. I am not going to jail. I have not done anything. I do not get into no trouble." I began to cry and called on the Name of Jesus. I even spoke in tongues. The officer must have been thinking, *this negro done lost her mind.*

"Mrs. Jackson, please calm down ma'am."

"No. You do not understand. I am a mother. I can't go to jail. Who is going to take care of my children? Please check the computer again. It must be wrong. Officer, please, please..."

"Mrs. Jackson. Calm down and listen to me. We have to resolve this problem."

"Okay, I'm listening." I was ready to hear a solution.

"You have a warrant. I can't do anything about it until you have been taken into custody. Once you have been arrested, we can investigate the matter further to find out what is going on. The reason for the warrant stated is that you did not appear in court; you are listed as a no-show."

"Court? For what?"

"In 2002."

Is this woman really talking about eight years ago? I explained, "The only thing I had eight years ago is traffic tickets and I paid them off."

"Well, that is all I know right now until you see the judge."

After hearing those words, my screaming and crying intensified. "I don't want to go to jail. I don't like jail!"

"Mrs. Jackson, I really believe you. Listen, the only thing I can do is..."

I thought she was about to say, *act like I never stopped your daughter,* but that was not the case.

"...give you until tomorrow at 1:00 p.m. to come to the police department. Ask for me and turn yourself in."

My thought was, *that is not helping me*, but I continued to listen.

"Meanwhile, contact a bondsman and post your bond ahead of time so that once you get to the police station, the process will go quickly. Can I trust you Mrs. Jackson? Unfortunately, there is no way around this. I am trying to help you. If you do not follow through with this agreement, I'm going to come looking for you and it won't be nice."

"Okay, okay. Tomorrow at one o'clock."

"Here is my number if you have any problems. If I do not see you by 1:00 p.m. our deal is off. Then I will have to come pick you up wherever I find you."

I agreed, "Okay. Tomorrow at one o'clock."

"Okay. I am releasing your daughter now. She is on her way home."

I sincerely thanked the officer and immediately texted my Apostle and the First Lady to let them know I would not be at church tonight and why. They replied. They planned to call me immediately after service and would be praying.

15
Fire

I prayed genuinely and specifically to God, "God, You know I don't like jail. Stop playing. This must be a test. There is no way I am going to jail. No, not jail. I know I told You before, 'Lord send me anywhere. Wherever You send me, I will go,' but let me change that. Lord, I will go anywhere but jail."

I called my friend Annette and told her everything. Like me, she could not believe it. She prayed for me and some of her words to the Lord were, "Lord, You know my friend don't like jail." That was a serious moment, but now looking back, I see the humor in her being led to pray the exact words I previously spoke to the Lord in private.

I did not call my mother because I did not want to upset her. This was all a mistake anyway, just a test of my faith.

After church, my Apostle and the First Lady called. They were very concerned. I explained from the beginning to the end what I had discussed with the officer. They advised me to follow the directions I received and to let them know what I needed help with. The First Lady offered to pick me up and to go with me at one o'clock to talk to the officer. *Thank God for great leaders.*

The next morning, I found a local bondsman in the yellow pages. I met him at his office and paid the bond. He explained to me what showed up on the computer. It said I previously had a court date scheduled concerning a traffic violation that I did not report to. That was all wrong. I brought the court copies of the old traffic tickets I already paid off years ago and my driver's license, which was still valid, with me. *This is a piece of cake; I can't wait to show them these papers*, I thought to myself. The bondsman went on to tell me that the justice system is known for messing up people like myself, "It is a shame that people have to go through unnecessary problems because somebody failed to do their job correctly."

I went home and prayed. I felt more confident now that I had the details regarding what I was facing and that it was *the system's fault.* The First Lady arrived around 12:30 p.m. The police department was only about ten minutes away from my house, so we arrived a little early. The First Lady remained calm and smiled beautifully as always, "Well, let's do this!"

We got out of the car. I called the officer on my cell phone to let her know I was at the police department. She said she was on her way and would arrive by one o'clock. We went into the building. I told the deputy at the front desk who I was there to see, that I had just spoken to her, and she was on her way.

The officer called my name as she entered the lobby. I approached her, she extended her hand, and we introduced ourselves. I introduced her to the First Lady and smiled as I reminded the officer, "I told you I was a Christian now!"

The officer directed us to follow her. The doors were buzzed for us to exit the lobby. We were led to a small room that only contained a telephone sitting on a desk and two chairs. Once we entered the room, the officer requested for us to close the door and have a seat. She explained what was going on.

I anxiously waited until she was done talking, then I showed her the paperwork I brought with me. "Officer, these are the actual copies of the records the court gave me in 2002 of my paid off traffic tickets. You can also verify that my driver's license is still valid. There is no way I could have a valid driver's license if I have unpaid traffic tickets." I was more than happy to provide the officer with my information. I was ready to get out of there.

"I understand everything you're saying, but there is a warrant in the system. The only person who can remove a warrant is a judge. Listen, I am going to call the dispatcher from right here on my radio just like if I had pulled you over. I'm going to give them your name, date of birth, and license number. If they advise me that you have a warrant, I am sorry, but I must arrest you."

I simply smiled and responded, "Okay." I had great faith. *Come on God, it is time for You to show up and to show out!*

We listened with great anticipation as the officer gave the dispatcher my information. The dispatcher responded using law enforcement codes. Then these words blared out from the radio as clear as day, "Warrant! Arrest suspect!"

There are no words to describe the shockwave that jolted through my body. *God, now where are You?*

The officer gestured towards the First Lady, "Mrs. Jackson, you can give her your jewelry now, so you don't have to deal with it once you get downtown to the main jail."

With water gathering in my eyes, I handed the First Lady my ring, earrings, and watch. While she was asking the officer some questions, I was asking God some questions: *God Why? What did I do? Why didn't You show up for me? I thought this was just a test!*

The First Lady did everything she could to stay strong in front of me and not breakdown, as tears rolled down my face. "I am going to wait around here to get as much information as possible. Don't worry, we will take care of the girls and make sure ShaTalya and Donajia get to and from school. Don't worry Sister Tawnya."

The officer respectfully said, "I'm not going to handcuff you as we walk through the building to the holding cell. I will take full responsibility for you. Will you please stand up?"

The First Lady was directed to exit the room and to call downtown to the main jail in a few hours in order to get additional information.

As I was walked through the building, all of the officers were looking at me. I was so ashamed. There I was, a Woman of God, who did not do anything to deserve this. I felt as if God had walked away from me. The door was buzzed for the cell to open. The officer sat me down and told me that she was really sorry about all of this.

I was in a small cell. The door slammed behind me, like an iron door in a dungeon. *Boom!* The sound was loud and terrifying. There I sat, on a hard bench looking at a stainless-steel toilet positioned in the middle of the floor. I cried and cried, then I prayed and cried. I could not believe this was really happening to me. I thought of when Paul and Silas were in prison. They prayed until the doors opened up. I kept praying and crying and looking but that cell door never opened.

16
Furnace

As I looked through the clear glass wall of the cell, I could see the desk where the two officers answered the phones and worked on their computers. The phones kept ringing and the two officers at the desk were so mean every time someone called to ask a question. They were so cold and callous. I did not want any part of those two.

Every now and then, the other inmates yelled from their cells and asked some of the craziest questions. The officers either ignored them or responded with an even crazier answer, like all this was just a game.

There was a big clock on the wall behind the desk where the officers were. It was torment as I watched the minutes of life, which some people take for granted, go by in slow motion.

About two hours passed. I listened as the officers talked on the phone about transferring three inmates to the county jail. There was a problem with the patty wagon. An officer was being sent in a patrol car to pick us up and then meet the patty wagon off I-95 and US Route 192 in a nightclub parking lot of all places. I was thinking,

Lord, this is a mess. God please hurry up and get me out of this situation. I continued to pray and cry.

Bam, Bam, Bam! The transport officer beat on the heavy metal door in the back of the police station. One of the officers left the desk to go open the door.

They took us out of the cells and handcuffed us one by one. The other two ladies were white. They were so stoned that they did not have a clue as to what was going on. Both of them were in car accidents earlier that day and arrested for Driving Under the Influence (D.U.I). I had always thought that meant drunk driving, but that day I learned it meant driving under the influence of *anything.* In their case, they were under the influence of oxycodone pills. There was not much logic to anything they said because they were still so high.

I was upset with God and continued to interrogate Him: *Okay God, why am I here again? What does this have to do with me? There must be something You are trying to show or teach me, but I do not see it.*

The transport officer was so nice to me. As he read over my paperwork on the clipboard he asked, "Why are you here? You don't look like you belong here." I started to explain, then he said, "I will tell someone to help you out when you get downtown so that this can be over for you ma'am." *Thank You Lord!*

After we drove about fifteen minutes we arrived at our destination. We pulled into the nightclub parking lot. As we got closer to the building, I noticed that there were at least twenty vehicles parked and people were standing all around them. *God, what is going on here? This is a nightclub. Why are all these men and little boys standing out here?*

The transport officer parked and told us he would be back in five to ten minutes. He had to give our paperwork to the receiving transport officer, then he would come back to remove us one by one.

While I waited and looked around, I concluded that this nightclub parking lot must have been the designated meeting place for a father and son camping trip. There were large coolers, sleeping bags, etc., tied on top of the vehicles. All the little boys were pointing to the police cars. I was so embarrassed. *God, You said You would never let me be put to shame. When I get out of this car in handcuffs, what will these people think of me? I look like some sort of criminal.* Yet again, I started to cry.

The officer returned and started to take us out of the patrol car one by one to the van. I was positioned to be the last one he took out. I prayed that the little boys and their fathers would be gone by the time the officer got to me, but that was not the case. They just stood there and stared as we walked to the van. Thankfully, when we got to the back of the van, we left their line of sight.

I had *the shock of my life* when I got to that van. They removed the handcuffs and put me in shackles and chains. My heart felt like it had just been pierced with a knife as tears ran uncontrollably down my face. The officer who had just taken over, tried to console me, "Ma'am, I'm sorry. The other officer told me about what happened to you. Even though this is all a mix up, this is part of the procedure that I must do." I nodded my head up and down. "When I get you there, I'm going to talk to someone so that you can be hurried through the process and get out." Again, I nodded my head up and down.

I was speechless. I kept asking myself and God, *what did I do to deserve this?* I remained very quiet and still as we rode to the main jail. Even the slightest movement produced a noise that made me sick to my stomach – it was the sound the chains that clung to me made as they scraped the floor of the van.

The other two ladies talked on and off. Their speech was slurred. They alternated between falling asleep and waking back up to continue their conversation right where they had left off. They were *tripping,* but who was I to be judging them, so I said a prayer in my heart for them.

We arrived at our designation and were escorted by officers into the building. Immediately they directed us to get up against the wall. The search process began in the open hallway. Right in the view of others, the officers touched us along the edge of our bras and pants. I felt humiliated and violated.

A bag of pills was found in one of the lady's bras; over one hundred pills. Now she was also being charged with trafficking and attempting to sell drugs in a jail. Her only response was, "How did that get there? That is not mine."

Oh my God! The officers were so nasty towards us. I asked, or more like told, the officer who searched me, "You don't have to be all rough with me! I'm not trying to give you a hard time."

She snapped back, "Who are you talking to?"

"You officer!" By this time I was more than a little fed up. I had stopped crying and got myself together. Saved and all, I have never been anybody's wimp.

"Just turn around!"

I turned around as she ordered and at the same time made it clear, through my posture and demeanor, that *Tawnya is not anyone's fool.*

The search was completed, and I was told to go have a seat until they call my name. The officers were in the middle of shift change. It was obvious, they were not in any rush to call names.

After sitting there for about an hour, I inquired, "Excuse me sir, when will I be able to use the phone?"

He responded, "After you finish getting processed. You just have to wait." So, I waited.

Finally, my name was called. The transport officer had been true to his word. Thankfully, he had already informed this officer about what was going on. He asked me for more information. I explained further to make sure he understood. Unfortunately, his response was the same, "There is no way around you being arrested. Once you get before the judge, you will have an opportunity to clear the charges."

They were willing to release me on my own recognizance and I had already posted my bond before I was arrested. With two ways out, I started to see past this moment of time. However, I still had to go through the whole fingerprinting and booking process which could take hours. The officer guaranteed I would be released that night. I was flooded with relief. *Thank You Lord!*

I finished all there was to do and was escorted to the holding cell. Eight other women were in there. They laid over the benches and on the floor of this dirty smelly small cell. Everyone looked like a big happy family. They shared their stories of how they ended up in their predicaments.

Two and a half hours passed, and I was given the opportunity to make a phone call. I called home to make sure my children were okay.

As I sat in that cold cell looking around, I knew this was never about me, but this had to be an assignment from the Lord. As I refocused, I saw more and more the great need for prayer for God's people. Some of the women among me were coming down off of all types of narcotics. The withdrawal effects of pills, cocaine, and other drugs had one woman vomiting and others rocking back and forth because they needed a fix.

My heart was stirred with compassion and I began to pray in my spirit for them. I was saddened to see so many young women and men coming to jail like it was a normal daily activity. The conversations they shared shed light to that fact. They talked about when they were here, just last week, for *this and that* charge.

After I spent several hours in the holding cell; they called my name. The time came for me to change my clothes and transition into the actual jail population. I had prayed hard that I would be released before I had to go in with the women who were serving time, but God was not finished with me yet in the jail.

I entered what looked like a big gymnasium with cots spread out everywhere. This set up was shockingly different than what I expected based on TV programs I watched in the past. I wrongfully assumed there would be two-person cells with iron metal doors. That was not the case at all.

The first correctional officer I encountered, as I walked in, was from my church. I did not know that she worked there. We were both surprised to see one another. She recognized me right away. "Hi. What is going on? Why are you here?"

I briefly explained and she encouraged me not to worry. I said to myself, *Thank you Lord for favor!*

Five to eight minutes later, I heard, "Mrs. Tawnya, what are you doing here?" I was so happy to see this young lady. She used to praise dance with my daughters and come over to my house all the time. I had not seen her in years, and I heard she had gotten in some trouble. I always kept a special place in my heart for her. I discerned such a sweet spirit and a great calling upon her life, so I knew why the enemy tried to fight against her. She walked over to my cot with several other young ladies and asked, "Why are you here?"

I began to tell my story again, for what felt like the *fiftieth* time. They all stood around anxiously listening to the details of my story. Moments after that, I heard someone say, "Don't I know you?"

I looked to the direction the voice came from. "Yes, honey. You have visited my church a few times. How are you doing?"

"Okay," she responded.

By this time everyone was getting ready for bed. Several people offered to help me make up my cot with the sheet, blanket, and pillowcase. I told them all, "No thank you! I am just passing through. I am not making up no bed."

We all prayed before going to bed. It was a blessing to see them gathered corporately for prayer. This was their nightly routine. They passed out the bible verses that they kept in a container and said them. Shortly after that, it was lights out.

My cot was against a wall. I sat on it and leaned my back against the wall. I continued to sit halfway up. I was determined not to lay down and go to sleep. I prayed for the women there and their families, children, and situations. I, *Mrs. Determination,* fell asleep sometime during my prayer.

About 3:45 a.m. my name was called on the intercom to go home. I woke up praising the Lord! I thanked God all the way to the door. One officer shushed me. The ladies started giggling and I heard a few whispers of goodbye.

I had gotten a few of the young ladies' addresses and told them I would keep in contact with them. As I left the jail, early that morning, I knew I would be a part of jail ministry one day. This whole thing was not about me, but it had everything to do with my Father's business. God wanted me to see the great need for prayer in the jail and prison system for His people.

When we tell God phrases like: *use me for Your Glory; have Your way in my life; and, God, I'll go wherever You want me to;* we better be ready. God's plans are not always nice and cute, but they will work together for our good!

Epilogue 2020

My Family

My mom is doing great. She lives with me and I am her caregiver. She has been diagnosed with several illnesses, but my family and I continue to believe God for her total healing. She gets around very well; walking, dressing herself, and is full of spunk.

My Daughters & Grandchildren

My oldest daughter Sha'Therian is 34 years old. She has an associate degree and is returning back to school to finish her bachelor's degree in Psychology. She has worked at a local Air Force base, in the Medical Department, for the past nine years. She has a 4-year-old daughter named Reya and has never been married.

My daughter Sha'Tawnya is 32 years old. She received her Pharmacy Tech Certification while she was in Job Corps. She also has an Associate Degree in Business Administration. She works in the Patient Services Department of a medical group. She has a 3-year-old daughter named Aaliyah and has never been married.

My daughter Sha'Talya is 27 years old and served 3 years in the U.S. Army. She has a barber license, obtained her Nursing Degree in 2017, earned a degree in Recording Arts in 2019, and in

December of 2020 she will also have a degree in Audio Engineering. She is the mother of three children: 7-year-old Kymani: 5-year-old King, and 1-year-old Kaden. She is married, but legally separated.

My youngest daughter Donajia is 18 years old. She is a senior in high school, an honor student, very independent, and responsible. She is such a sweet spirited person.

Me

I am the owner of 'A Taste of T's Delicacy', which is a catering business. October 2014, I was ordained as a Prophetess of God. The same year, God laid upon my heart to start a 5 a.m. prayer line, which is still active today. From 2015-2019, I led a prayer ministry. We routinely gathered together at 6 a.m. on Melbourne Beach to pray.

I genuinely thank you for reading my first book, *My Story, How God Delivered, Healed, and Set Me Free*. My second book titled, *The Conclusion of My Story*, will be available 2022. I would love to hear from you. If you have a prayer request to share or would like to partner for conferences, special events, book clubs, or study groups, please email me at TawnyaJackson0@gmail.com.

**My Parents in the 1980's
Cephas & Willie Dean
Brooks**

**My Mom, 2020
God's Miracle**

**Me – Enjoying
Deliverance,
Healing, & Freedom**

My Family

**My Grandchildren
2020
King, Kayden,
Kymani, Reya,
& Aaliyah**

**Me & My Four Beloved
Daughters All Grown Up**

Fuel
10-Day Devotional

Through it all, it was God Himself who delivered, healed, and set me free.

Through it all, it is God Himself who delivers, heals, and sets me free.

Through it all, it was God Himself who delivered, healed, and set you free.

Through it all, it is God Himself who delivers, heals, and sets you free.

I would like to share with you twenty bible verses that kept me and shined light into my darkest days. They continue to enlighten and inspire me to move forward in everything God has for me.

I ask that you set forth on a ten-day journey of meaningful devotion using the journal provided in the upcoming pages. My prayer is that you are also empowered to experience and share your personal testimony of deliverance, healing, and freedom; to provide hope and strength to others.

Day 1: *Purpose*

Before I formed thee in the belly I knew thee; and before thou camest forth out of the womb I sanctified thee, and I ordained thee a prophet unto the nations.
Jeremiah 1:5

O taste and see that the LORD is good: blessed is the man that trusteth in him.
Psalm 34:8

What is God saying to you through these verses?

_____
_____
_____
_____
_____
_____
_____

What is your response?

_____
_____
_____
_____
_____
_____
_____
_____
_____
_____
_____
_____

Day 2:

Thy word have I hid in mine heart, that I might not sin against thee.
                                                    Psalm 119:11

I love the Lord, because he hath heard my voice and my supplications.
                                                    Psalms 116:1

What is God saying to you through these verses?

_____
_____
_____
_____
_____
_____
_____

What is your response?

_____
_____
_____
_____
_____
_____
_____
_____
_____
_____
_____
_____

Day 3: *Forgiveness*

Be not overcome of evil, but overcome evil with good.

Romans 12:21

But I say unto you which hear, Love your enemies, do good to them which hate you, Bless them that curse you, and pray for them which despitefully use you.

Luke 6:27-28

What is God saying to you through these verses?

What is your response?

Day 4:

Now faith is the substance of things hoped for, the evidence of things not seen.
                                        Hebrews 11:1

For we walk by faith, not by sight.
                                        2 Corinthians 5:7 NKJV

What is God saying to you through these verses?

_____
_____
_____
_____
_____
_____
_____

What is your response?

_____
_____
_____
_____
_____
_____
_____
_____
_____
_____
_____
_____
_____

Day 5: *Patience*

My brethren, count it all joy when ye fall into divers temptations; Knowing this, that the trying of your faith worketh patience. But let patience have her perfect work, that ye may be perfect and entire, wanting nothing.

James 1:2-4

Wait on the LORD: be of good courage, and he shall strengthen thine heart: wait, I say, on the LORD.

Psalm 27:14

What is God saying to you through these verses?

_____
_____
_____
_____
_____
_____
_____
_____

What is your response?

_____
_____
_____
_____
_____
_____
_____
_____
_____
_____
_____
_____
_____
_____

Day 6:

And he said unto me, My grace is sufficient for thee: for my strength is made perfect in weakness. Most gladly therefore will I rather glory in my infirmities, that the power of Christ may rest upon me.
2 Corinthians 12:9

Therefore, my beloved brethren, be ye stedfast, unmoveable, always abounding in the work of the Lord, forasmuch as ye know that your labour is not in vain in the Lord.
1 Corinthians 15:58

What is God saying to you through these verses?

___

What is your response?

___

Day 7: *Comfort*

And Jesus said unto them, I am the bread of life: he that cometh to me shall never hunger; and he that believeth on me shall never thirst.

John 6:35

God is our refuge and strength, a very present help in trouble.

Psalm 46:1

What is God saying to you through these verses?

_____
_____
_____
_____
_____
_____
_____

What is your response?

_____
_____
_____
_____
_____
_____
_____
_____
_____
_____
_____
_____

Day 8: *Confidence*

Cast not away therefore your confidence, which hath great recompence of reward.

Hebrews 10:35

And blessed is she that believed: for there shall be a performance of those things which were told her from the Lord.

Luke 1:45

What is God saying to you through these verses?

_____
_____
_____
_____
_____
_____
_____

What is your response?

_____
_____
_____
_____
_____
_____
_____
_____
_____
_____
_____
_____
_____
_____

Day 9: Restoration

The LORD is my rock, and my fortress, and my deliverer; my God, my strength, in whom I will trust; my buckler, and the horn of my salvation, and my high tower.

Psalm 18:2

Death and life are in the power of the tongue: and they that love it shall eat the fruit thereof.

Proverbs 18:21

What is God saying to you through these verses?

What is your response?

Day 10: Prosperity

Beloved, I wish above all things that thou mayest prosper and be in health, even as thy soul prospereth.

3 John 1:2

By humility and the fear of the LORD are riches, and honour, and life.

Proverbs 22:4

What is God saying to you through these verses?

_____
_____
_____
_____
_____
_____
_____
_____

What is your response?

_____
_____
_____
_____
_____
_____
_____
_____
_____
_____
_____
_____

www.ingramcontent.com/pod-product-compliance
Lightning Source LLC
Chambersburg PA
CBHW071907070526
44583CB00016B/1882